G-BUGS
THE GRATITUDE BUGS™

Sam Meets Caterpillar Kaleb

Written and Created by **Jackie Jones**

Illustrated by **George Athanasiou**

Edited by **Mike Muxlow**

Jackie Jones

ACCEPTANCE GRATEFULNESS SELF-ESTEEM HONESTY INTEGRITY RESPONSIBILITY RESPECT FORGIVENESS LOYALTY FRIENDSHIP

In memory of my Dad
(happy faces)

For my dear Mother, wonderful husband, brothers and sisters,
the in-laws, the "outlaw", our amazing kids and beautiful grandchildren.

With loving gratitude

Foreword

One of life's greatest lessons is in learning to be grateful for what we have. This is also one of the hardest to teach in this time of extravagance, easy access to luxuries, constant advances in technology, and a mentality of "more is better".

Combine this with pressures on family time and it is easy to see why this particular life lesson may be ignored or forgotten. As parents, we are ultimately responsible for ensuring our children develop the skills required to become happy, productive, contributing adults. True happiness eludes those who haven't learned the lessons of gratitude. There will always be someone that has more, often much more. More money, more friends, more gadgets, better clothes, a better job and better health. There will also always be someone that has less, often much less. Teaching your child to create their own definitions for happiness and success is one of the greatest gifts you can give.

When Jackie first told me of The Gratitude Bugs, over coffee of course, it brought tears to my eyes and gave me chills. Everyone, even those with "differences" should have the magic of gratitude in their lives. Sam and The Gratitude Bugs can be part of teaching this life lesson and will initiate important conversations in your family for years to come. For that we can all feel grateful!

Karen Melnick *RN, BSN, Award-winning Author:* Your Child's Health & Wellness Record
www.healthandwellnessrecord.com

'Squeak!'

"What was that cheerful squeaking sound?" Sam asked himself. He had never heard that noise before.

Sam was curious so he put down his truck and listened carefully as he tiptoed over to the garden.

'Squeak!'

There it was again. Sam went closer and suddenly, something moved!

Reaching towards a swaying leaf, he slowly turned it over. Clinging to the back was a cute and fuzzy caterpillar.

Sam carefully picked up the caterpillar and placed it in his hand.

As it crawled, Sam giggled. Its tiny legs were tickling his hand.

After watching for a few seconds, Sam noticed that the caterpillar walked differently than any caterpillar he'd seen before.

It bumped up and down.
This caterpillar had a limp!

Sam began petting its soft, furry body and after a few strokes, the caterpillar started to make a squeaking noise.

"Squeak, squeak, squeak."
Then suddenly, it began to speak!

"Hey there, *'squeak'*, little man. That, *'squeak'*, tickles!" Sam's eyes grew big with surprise! He didn't know what to say.

The caterpillar spoke again. "I'm Caterpillar Kaleb. *'Squeak'*. What's your name little man?"

Sam gulped and answered. "I'm Sam."

“I think I’ll call you, *‘squeak’*, Little Man Sam,” replied the caterpillar.

Sam smiled and thought his new nickname was pretty cool.

He looked Caterpillar Kaleb in the eye and asked, “Why do you walk with a limp?”

Caterpillar Kaleb responded confidently, "I, *'squeak'*, was born this way. One of my front legs is shorter than the rest. I waited for it to grow, *'squeak'*, but it never did, so I limp when I walk."

"That's too bad," said Sam. "Does it bother you that you're not like the other caterpillars?"

Caterpillar Kaleb told Sam that he used to feel sorry for himself and that the other bugs teased him because he was different.

“I was embarrassed to go into the, *‘squeak’*, garden to play, so I hid by the rock at the garden’s edge. It was lonely there and I never had much fun, *‘squeak’*, all by myself,” replied the caterpillar.

"Then one day," Caterpillar Kaleb said happily, "I was tired of feeling sad, *'squeak'*, and alone so I mustered up all my courage, *'squeak'*, and I went into the garden with the other bugs.

And you know what, *'squeak'*,
happened Little Man Sam?"
the furry caterpillar asked.

"What?" said Sam anxiously.

"I realized that although I have one short leg, all my other legs are perfectly fine.

I also felt lucky that I could, *'squeak'*, get around at all because some bugs have more, *'squeak'*, troubles than me," explained Sam's fuzzy new friend.

"Like the bugs on my Dad's windshield?" asked Sam.

"Well, not quite like that," laughed Caterpillar Kaleb.

“I have a bumblebee friend whose, *‘squeak’*, little brother has trouble getting around on his own.

He has a condition called autism and the whole family, *‘squeak’*, watches him very closely so he doesn’t get lost or hurt,” explained Caterpillar Kaleb.

"Ahh-tism?" questioned Sam.

"Yeah, that's right. His brain doesn't work the same as most other bees so he can't be left alone," answered Caterpillar Kaleb.

"That's why I'm grateful that I can walk on my own whenever I want," squeaked the caterpillar. "And now I have lots of friends and nobody, *'squeak'*, teases me anymore. I'm happy all the time and try to think good thoughts every day," he added.

Sam was also happy for Caterpillar Kaleb and knew this was the start of a special friendship.

"Would you like to meet my, *'squeak'*, friends sometime Little Man Sam?" asked the caterpillar.

"That would be so great!" exclaimed Sam excitedly.

"Okay then, I think they'd like to, *'squeak'*, meet you too," replied Caterpillar Kaleb.

Before Sam made his way back to his toys he had one more thing he wanted to say to his new friend "Can I tell you something?" asked Sam.

"Sure, I'm all ears," squeaked Caterpillar Kaleb.

"You mean you're all legs," said Sam giggling. "I'm very glad I met you today and I hope I see you again soon," he added.

As Sam skipped towards his house he thought, “I think I’ll call Caterpillar Kaleb my ‘Gratitude Bug’ - he’s grateful he can walk and I’m grateful that I have a friend like him.”

Get more gratitude bugs at ***g-bugs.com***